MAKING
Shoes

MAKING Shoes

RUTH THOMSON
PHOTOGRAPHY: CHRIS FAIRCLOUGH

FRANKLIN WATTS
LONDON/NEW YORK/SYDNEY/TORONTO

Copyright © 1987 Franklin Watts

Franklin Watts Inc
387 Park Avenue South
New York, N.Y. 10016

US ISBN: 0–531–10444–3
Library of Congress Catalog
Card No: 87–50450

Printed in Belgium

Design: Edward Kinsey
Illustrations: Kathleen McDougall

The publisher, author and
photographer would like to
thank C and J Clark of Street,
England, for their kind
permission to undertake this
book.

CONTENTS

DN

TAKE A CLOSER LOOK

Next time you put on a pair of shoes, stop to have a closer look at them. Can you believe that each pair is made over a period of five days and that more than 25 people have a hand in making them?

The shoes are made of two parts – the soles that you walk upon and the uppers which surround your feet. In the photograph you can see all the pieces (except for the sole) which are used to make just *one* shoe. They all have to be fitted together in the right order.

▷ The parts of a shoe

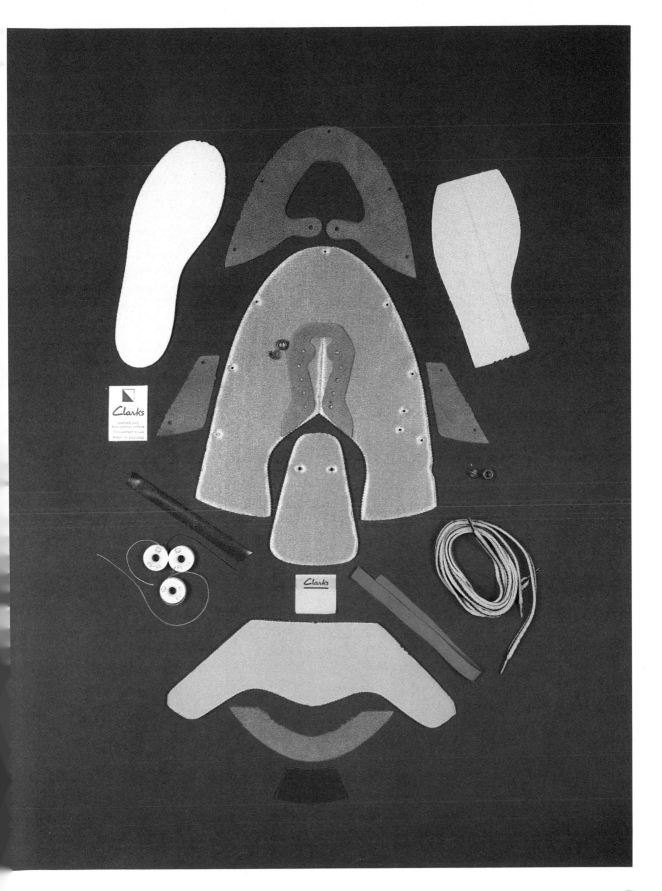

MAKING THE UPPERS

Shoes are made in batches of twelve pairs at a time, all the same size and fitting. Each batch is kept together throughout its manufacture, with a clearly marked ticket.

The uppers are made mostly from foam-backed nylon. Six pieces have been stapled together so that the cutter can cut several vamps (the front piece of the upper) at one time.

He positions a knife on the nylon and swings the hydraulic press over it. He touches two pads and the pressure pushes the knife down, right through all the layers of material.

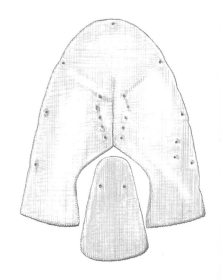

▽ The uppers are cut from sheets of foam-backed nylon.

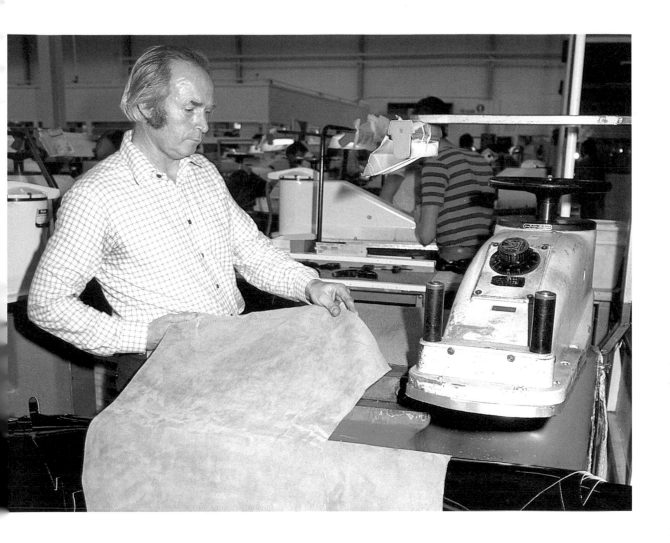

The leather suede trimming is cut into five different pieces for each shoe, and each has to be cut separately. Leather suede, unlike nylon, can stretch and may have marks or faults in it. The cutter positions the knives with care, so that he makes best use of the leather suede and avoids any of the blemishes.

The knives are clearly marked with the design number of the shoe style and their size. The tabs are color coded for different width fittings. Yellow and blue tabs, for example, mean F and G fittings.

△ Leather suede is used for the shoe trimmings.

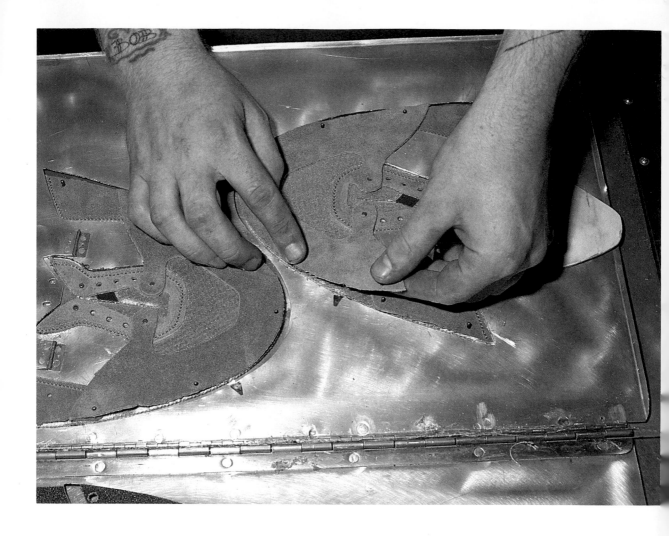

△ The nylon vamps and the leather suede trimmings are fitted together before stitching.

▽ The underneath edge of the leather suede is trimmed to make it less bulky to stitch.

Each pair of vamps is fitted into a metal frame called a pallet. Now you can see why the vamps have little holes all around them. They are positioning holes which fit on to pins in the pallet. These hold the vamps in place while they are being stitched. If the pieces moved at all, the stitching would be very uneven.

Each suede piece is fitted in its correct position on top of the vamp. Once all the pieces are in place, the pallet is closed and locked firmly with clips.

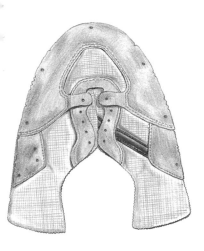

The pallet is fitted under an automatic sewing machine. The machine is computer controlled. It stitches on the suede in exactly the way it has been programmed to do. This kind of stitching would be much more difficult to do by hand – it would be hard to keep it consistent.

The machine operator uses two pallets. While one is under the machine, he takes out the stitched vamps from the other pallet. He replaces them with all the pieces for another pair. This pallet is ready for stitching just as the machine finishes stitching the first pair. In this way, no time is wasted.

▽ An automatic sewing machine is used to sew the trimmings and vamp.

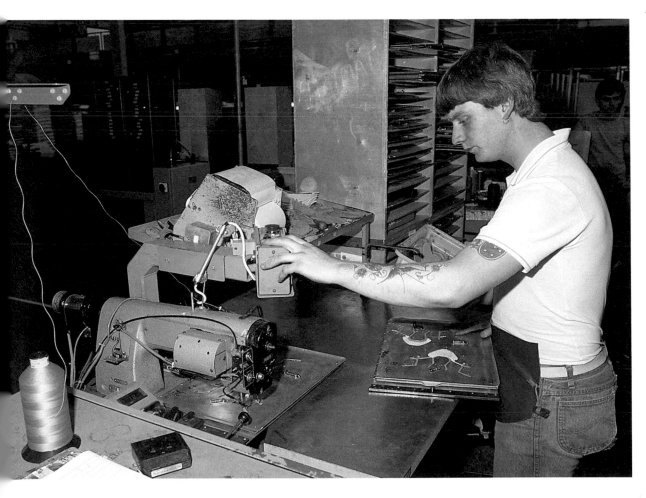

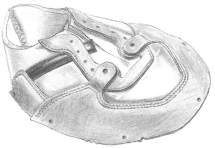

The two ends of the vamp are sewn together with strong zig-zag stitching. While they are being stitched, the tongues are being sewn separately.

◁ The ends of the vamps are sewn together. Can you see how the uppers are beginning to take shape?

▽ The tongues are also stitched together at this stage.

The machinist covers the edges on three sides with cloth binding, to stop them from fraying. She does this in one continuous movement, attaching the next tongue, as soon as she finishes binding the previous one.

When she has bound a whole batch of twenty-four tongues, she snips between each one to separate it and trim off any surplus tape.

A label with Clark's name is stitched on over the end of the tongue. Now the tongues are ready to be joined to the uppers.

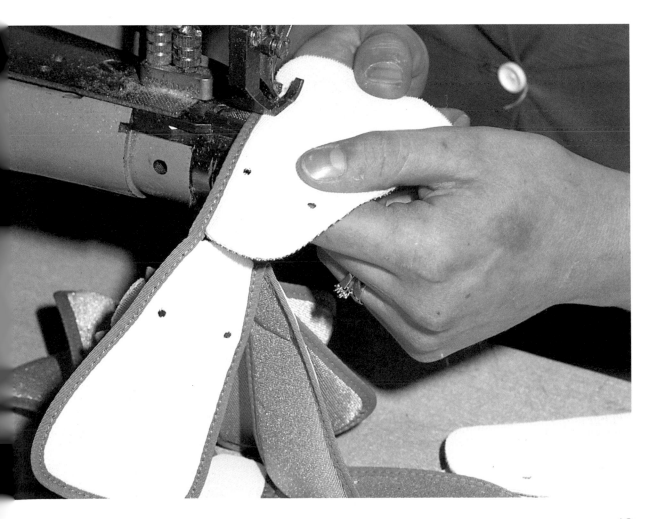

A machinist attaches a little cherry-colored logo over the back of the vamps. This hides part of the zig-zag stitching and strengthens the back of the shoe. Next, she sews the collar (heel) lining on to the back of the shoe and turns it to the inside. This lining makes the shoe comfortable to wear.

Finally, she stitches on top of the parts she has already sewn together. This is called topstitching. It is stitching that you can see.

The shoes are run through a blade which vibrates very quickly. Extra material, which might otherwise rub the feet when the shoes are worn, is trimmed away.

△ The lining is joined to the outside of the shoes and then turned to the inside and stitched in place.

▷ Extra material is trimmed away.

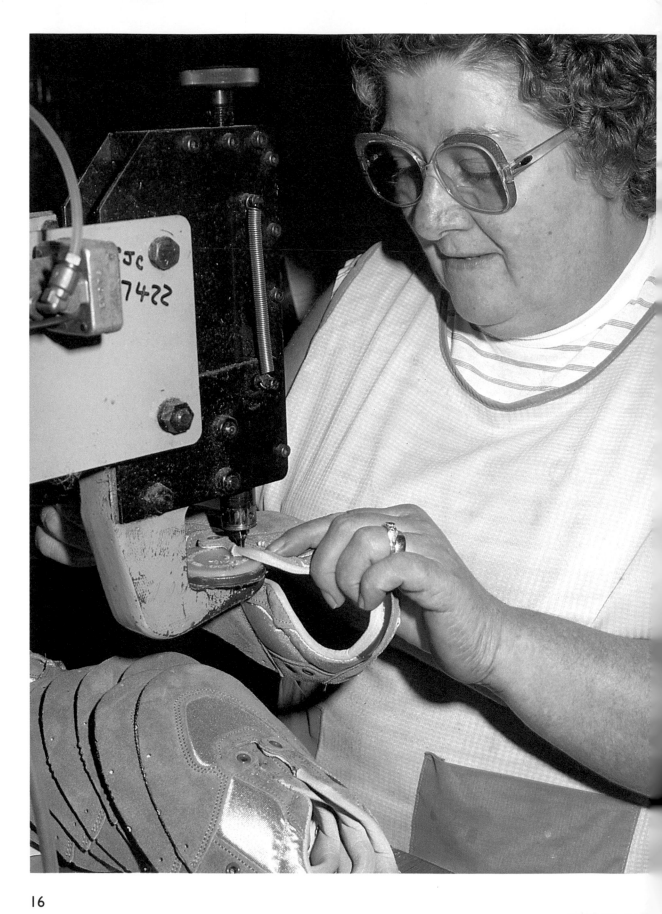

◁ Holes are punched for the lacing holes.

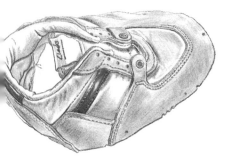

◁ Holes are punched for
the lacing holes.

Next a person punches lacing holes and puts eyelets in the shoes. While the vamps were still flat (before they were joined at the back) she punched two breathing hole eyelets on the inside edge.

In the photograph below, she is putting eyelets on the top two lacing holes. The machine punches a hole. An eyelet drops over the hole and she presses a foot-pedal to press it into place.

She uses another machine to punch and clean the other lacing holes which do not have eyelets. Now the shoes are ready to have their tongues attached.

▽ Metal eyelets are put in
the top two lacing holes.

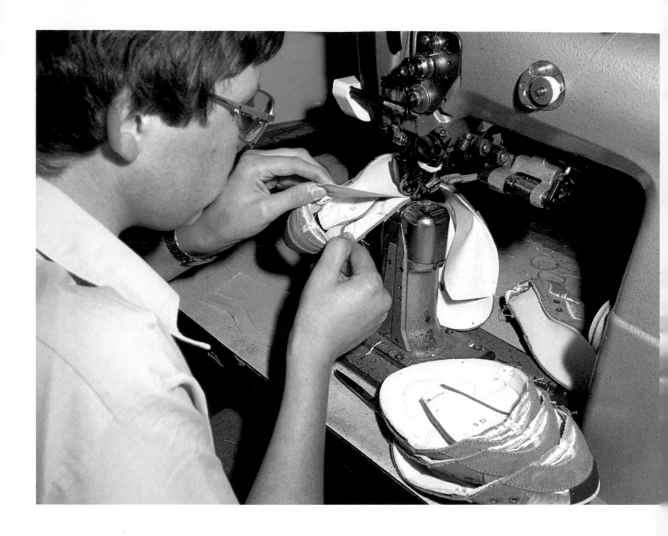

A canvas sock is sewn on to the bottom of each upper. This gives the shoe its shape.

Another machinist attaches two long strings on to each toe. These will be used, later, to pull the toe into shape. She leaves a long length of string on one side of the toe and runs the toe through this overlocking machine. This binds the string securely to the toe. She leaves an equally long length on the other side, before snipping it off.

Now the batch of uppers is finished (closed, to use the shoemaker's term). The shoes are taken to the molding room where the soles will be put on.

△ Stitching the canvas sock to the upper.

▷ The uppers are finished when the strings are attached to the toes.

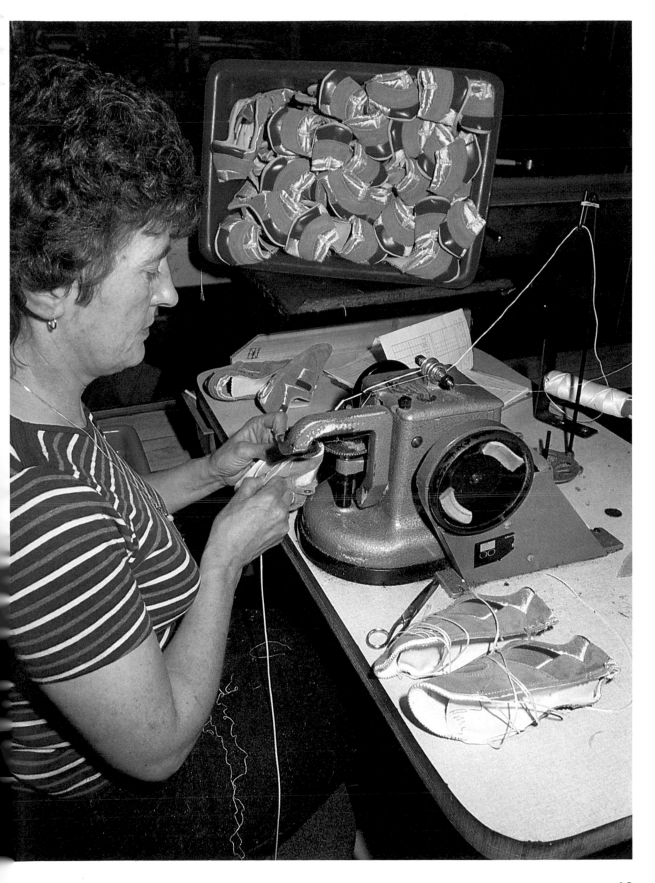

MOLDING THE SOLES

The soles are put on to the uppers in another building of the shoe factory, which houses several enormous molding machines. Each machine has twelve revolving "stations" in which any size and shape of shoe can be molded.

When a batch of shoes is brought for molding, the right and left feet are sorted and separated. The correct size mold is fitted into an empty mold box. The mold is made up of three pieces – two side pieces and a sole. The correct last (model of a foot) is fixed to the end of a pillar, above the box.

▷ A molding machine.

▽ The mold and last.

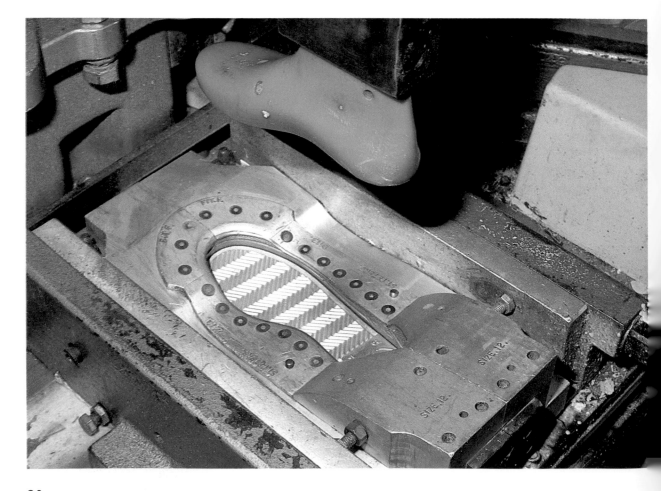

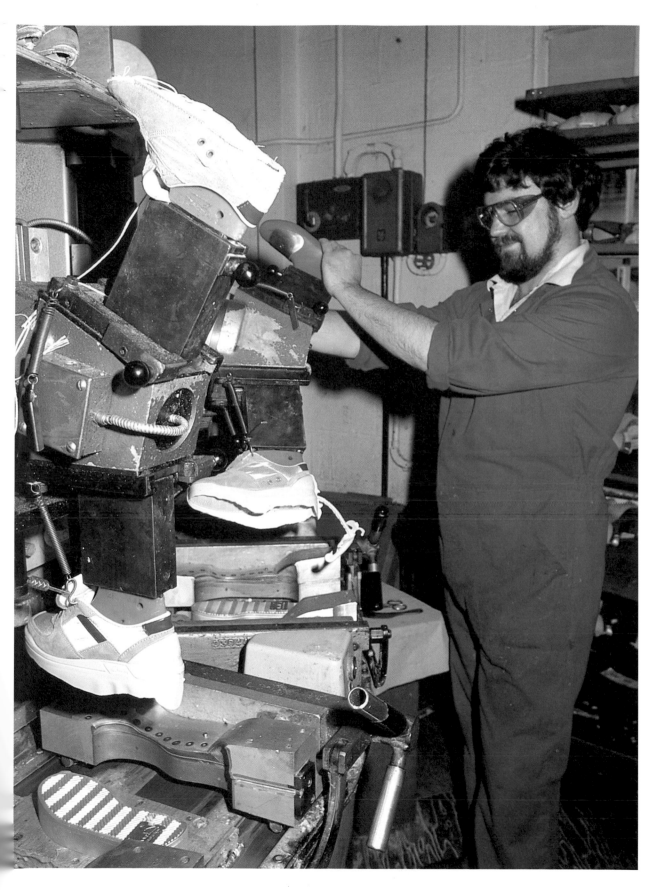

The machine operator drapes a shoe over the last and pulls the strings on the toe. He twists them around a T-bar to help him pull them as tight as possible. In doing so, he gives the toe its final, proper shape.

Once he has done this, he turns the pillar over and lowers the shoe into the mold box. He makes sure that the shoe is correctly positioned, fixes the front with a spring fastening and closes the mold.

The "station" moves around until the mold box is opposite the injection head of the chemical tanks.

△ Strings are used to pull the shoe into shape.

▽ The mold is waxed before each molding.

Two chemicals are mixed together to produce the material for the soles. A controlled amount of chemicals is squirted, at high pressure, through a tiny hole into the mold box.

The mixture is hot and extremely sticky. It expands in the mold box and sticks easily on to the rough surfaces of the suede and canvas parts of the shoe. It sets very fast.

After six minutes, the mold is opened, the last is lifted out and the "tail" on the shoe is cut off. The pillar is turned over so that another shoe can be put into the mold and the finished one is left to harden.

▽ The upper being molded to the sole.

THE FINISHING TOUCHES

◁ The ragged ends of the sole are cut off.

The shoe is trimmed all the way around to give the molding a smooth edge. The blade of the knife vibrates so fast you cannot see it moving. Now you can see the shoe's final shape.

The inside of each sole is brushed with glue and a foam sock is firmly stuck into place. Then a sticky label is printed on to the heel of the sock. The label gives the name of the manufacturer, the materials from which the shoe was made and the country where it was made.

▽ The foam socks are glued on.

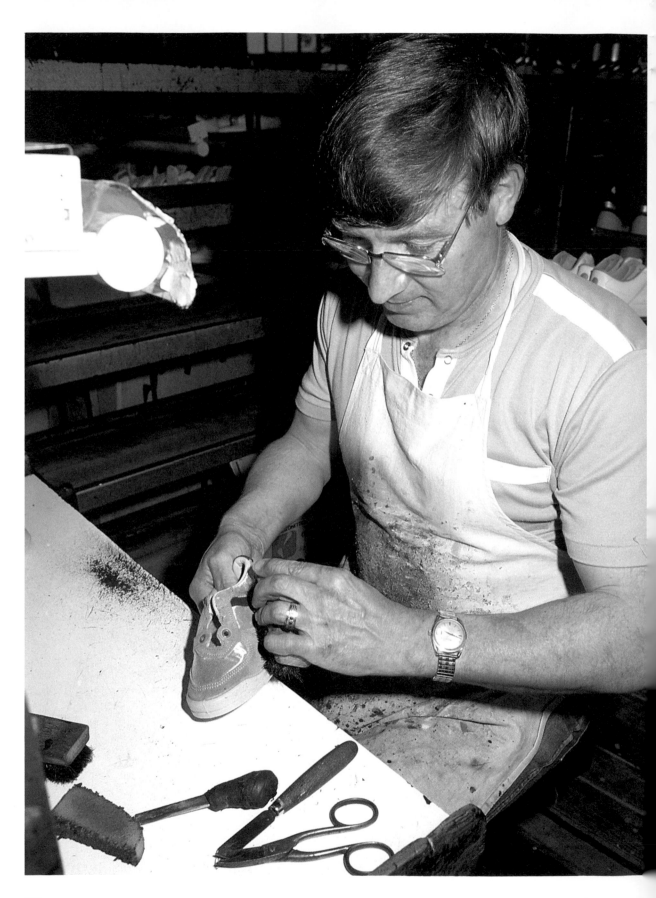

◁ Cleaning and finishing the shoe.

The finisher gives the shoes their final touches. He snips off any loose threads with scissors and trims away any excess bits of lining with a knife. The finisher then cleans off any dirty marks on the molding with a sponge and buffs the suede with a wire brush.

The very last process is the painting of a thin, red decorative line all the way round the outside edge of the sole. Ink drips through the nozzle of a thin tube. The shoe is held close to the nozzle and move around to allow the ink to flow evenly along the line.

▽ Painting the red line around the sole.

Now this batch of shoes is completely finished. A quality control inspector thoroughly examines each pair. Look at the checklist to see all the things he looks for. From long experience, he can immediately spot if something is wrong or missing.

Only if everything on his checklist is satisfactory are the shoes allowed through to the packing department.

Checklist
* Are the shoes a pair?
* Are they marked with the correct size and fit?
* Do the color shades match?
* Are the depths of the toes the same?
* Are the depths of the vamps the same?
* Is there any stitching missing on the front facing?
* Is the stitching on the back right?
* Is there any stitch missing around the lacing holes?
* Are the heights of the back molding the same?
* Is there any dirt on the outside of the vamps?
* Are there any mistakes in the molding?
* Are the socks properly stuck on?
* Is the Clarks label square?
* Have the linings been properly trimmed?
* Is the painted line around the edge of the sole right?

▷ The quality control inspector checking to see that the heights of the back molding are the same.

Each pair of shoes is laced, folded in tissue paper and packed into a box, along with an extra pair of laces. A special computer card is also put into each box. When a shop sells a box of shoes, it returns the card to automatically re-order another pair of shoes of that particular style and size.

The boxes are labeled and tied up in batches, ready to be sent to shoe stores.

△ Every shoe box has a label which describes the style, the size and width of the shoes inside.

29

THE PROCESS AT A GLANCE

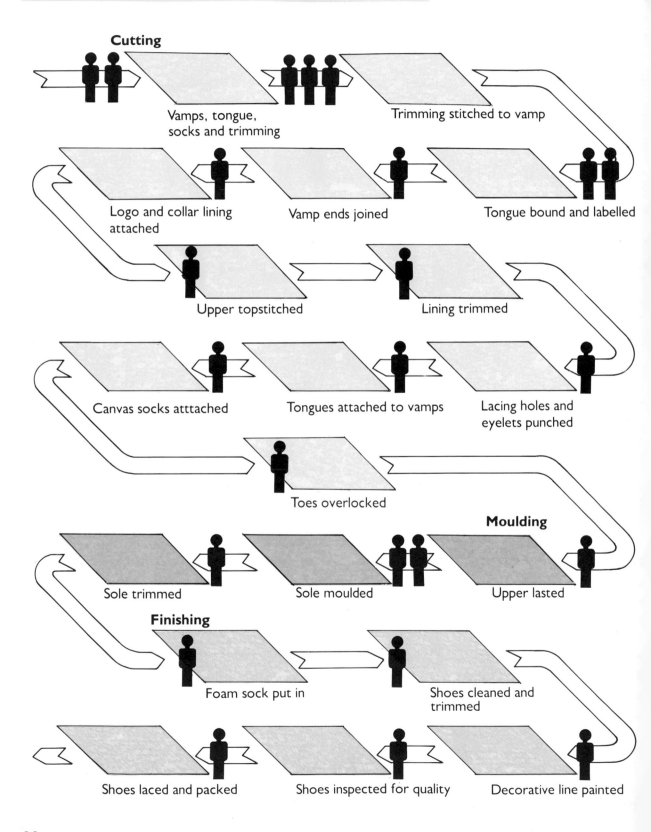

Cutting

Vamps, tongue, socks and trimming

Trimming stitched to vamp

Logo and collar lining attached

Vamp ends joined

Tongue bound and labelled

Upper topstitched

Lining trimmed

Canvas socks atttached

Tongues attached to vamps

Lacing holes and eyelets punched

Toes overlocked

Moulding

Sole trimmed

Sole moulded

Upper lasted

Finishing

Foam sock put in

Shoes cleaned and trimmed

Shoes laced and packed

Shoes inspected for quality

Decorative line painted

FACTS ABOUT SHOES

The first shoes were probably pieces of animal hide that cavemen wrapped around their feet to keep them from becoming frozen or bruised. Since then, people have worn a vast range of different types and styles of shoe.

In the United States today, at least 5,000 styles, types and sizes of shoes are made. A single shoe manufacturer may produce up to 60 styles with 90 size and width variations in each style.

Shoes were seen as a mark of rank or status until mass-production began in the 19th century. Some styles in the Middle Ages were so fanciful that the wearer had difficulty in walking!

Shoe manufacture began to be mechanized with the invention of the sewing machine by Elias Howe (1819–1897). Howe's machine could only stitch the shoe uppers. A machine to stitch the upper to the soles was designed by the American shoe manufacturer, Lyman Reed Blake (1835–1883). Blake's patent for the machine was brought by Gordon McKay

(1821–1903) and installed in his factory. This was the beginning of the manufacture of shoes in both the United States and the World.

Vulcanized rubber has been increasingly used for footwear in the 20th century. Synthetic rubber, discovered during World War II, by Dr. Waldo Semon, is now the most important shoe-making material, giving hardwearing waterproof soles. Plastics are much used for uppers.

Some types of shoes:

Ballroom dancing shoes
Ballet shoes
Tap dancing shoes
Slippers
Clogs
Cowboy boots
Wellington boots
Riding boots
Waders
Moccasins
Desert boots
Fell boots
Galoshes
Overshoes
Badminton shoes
Baseball boots
Basketball boots
Bowling shoes
Boxing shoes

Climbing boots
Cricket shoes
Curling shoes
Cycling shoes
Football boots
Hiking shoes
Jogging shoes
Lacrosse shoes
Shooting boots
Skating boots
Golf shoes
Ski boots
Squash shoes
Tennis shoes
Training shoes
Wrestling boots
Yachting shoes
Surgical boots
Mules
Espadrilles
Evening shoes
Safety boots
Work boots
Pumps
Flip-flops
Water (jelly) shoes

INDEX

PRINTED IN BELGIUM BY
proost
INTERNATIONAL BOOK PRODUCTION

DUE